String Algorithms for the day before your coding interview

Aditya Chatterjee x Ue Kiao

iq.OPENGENUS.org

Introduction

Strings are fundamental data type in real world and developing algorithms to deal with it is an important domain. In interviews, often, **string-based algorithms are most insightful and challenging**.

In this guide for the day before your coding interview, we have explored some problems and **demonstrated the thought process** to solve it starting from the brute force solutions.

In the process, we have **covered all fundamental ideas** along with applying Dynamic Programming to String algorithms so that you are able to solve all string-based problems.

Some of the problems we have covered are:

- **Check substring**: This is an important fundamental problem where we learn how strings can be handled just like numeric data and algorithms for numeric data can be leveraged.

  Some of the core concepts we explored are **string hashing**, **rolling hash** and much more.

- **Longest common substring**: This is a core problem as this uses the concepts we gained in the previous problems and an alternative solution is to use Dynamic Programming.
  The core idea is to apply Dynamic Programming over two different string data.

- **Longest repeating substring**: In line with our previous problem, we explored how to apply Dynamic Programming for this problem. The key distinction is that we are dealing with just 1 string instead of 2 strings as in the previous problem. Unlike the previous problem, the Dynamic Programming approach is the only optimal solution.

With these problems and the thought process to solve them, you will be fully prepared.

Book: **String Algorithms for the day before your coding interview**

Authors: Aditya Chatterjee, Ue Kiao.

Published: May 2020

Publisher: OpenGenus.

Series: Day before Coding Interview

Contact: team@opengenus.org

Let us get started with our first problem directly.

Other books you must read

- [Problems on Array: For Interviews and Competitive Programming](#)

- [Binary Tree Problems: Must for Interviews and Competitive Coding](#)

- [Time Complexity Analysis](#)

- [Dynamic Programming on Trees](#)

- [Day before Coding Interview](#) series

- [#7daysOfAlgo](#) series

Problem 1: Check sub-string

While solving this problem, we will learn two fundamental ideas of handling strings:

- **String hashing**: Representing strings as integers
- **Rolling hashing**: Generate string hash of all sub-strings efficiently

This will give you ideas on how to handle string as an integer data. This is significant because:

- Comparing integers takes place in near constant time (exact details further in this problem)
- We can leverage algorithms that work on Integer data

The problem is that we need to check if a given string S1 is a sub-string of another string S2. This might seem to be a simple problem but, solving this efficiently requires deep understanding of string comparisons. We will learn about rolling hash technique while we go through this.

Before we go any further, let us understand the problem.

A string S1 is a sub-string of another string S2 if S2 contains S1. For example:

If S1 = ENG and S2 = OPENGENUS, then S1 is a sub-string of S2.

OPENGENUS

If S1 = EGU and S2 = OPENGENUS, then S1 is not a sub-string of S2 as the word EGU does not occur continuously in S2.

Pause and think for a couple of minutes before proceeding further.

The basic approach that will come to your head is to compare the sub-string S1 with sub-strings of S1 of the same length. Consider the length of S1 to be N1.

Then, potential sub-strings of S2 will be:

{ S2[i], ..., S2[i+N1] } for every i = 0 to N-N1

The pseudocode of this approach will be as follows:

```
int length1 = length(string1)
int length2 = length(string2)

for i from 0 to length1 - length2 + 1
    for j from i to i+length2-1
        if string1[j] == string2[j-i]
            break
        // string matched at this point (if reached)
```

The catch is that comparing two strings takes linear time O(N) and not constant time O(1). Pause here and think about this as this is a key idea. Compare it with Integer comparison.

To solve this problem efficiently, we need to reduce the comparison time to O(1) and the only way to do so is to convert string to an integer and then, compare the integers.

Hence, there are two sub-steps:

- Convert string to integer
- Compare the integers

One point to note here is that you need to convert every unique string to an unique integer. This is a classical hashing problem. One common yet effective approach to convert a string to integer is as follows:

- Chose a prime number say P
- For a string S, the integer will be H

$$H = S[0] * P^0 + S[1] * P^1 + S[2] * P^2 + ... + S[N-1] * P^{N-1}$$

For example, take the string "AC" and the prime to be 3, then the integer will be:

$$H = A * 1 + C * 3$$

$$H = 65 + 67 * 3 = 266$$

With this, you understand that we can compare strings in constant time with this approach.

To understand this point deeper, go through this article:

iq.opengenus.org/string-hashing/ at OpenGenus

Note that converting a string of length N to an integer takes linear time O(N). To solve our problem, we need to tackle this. The solution to this is known as rolling hash.

Let us try to understand how we can improve this. Think of how we are getting the potential sub-strings.

{ S2[i], ..., S2[i+N1] } for every i = 0 to N-N1

Consider the ith substring to be S_i and $i+1^{th}$ substring to be S_j. Note both are consecutive substrings. If you observe closely, you will notice that following:

- Only 2 characters differ in S_i and S_j
- First character of S_i is missing in S_j
- Last character of S_j is missing in S_i
- The remaining characters are same in S_i and S_j

We need to take the advantage of this in the conversion of string to integer.

$$Si = S2[i], S2[i+1], ..., S2[i+N-1]$$

$$Sj = S2[i+1], S2[i+2], ..., S2[i+N-1], ..., S2[i+N]$$

So, $\mathbf{H(Si)} = S[i] * P^0 + S[i+1] * P^1 + S[i+2] * P^2 + ... + S[i+N-1] * P^{N-1}$

Similarly, $\mathbf{H(Sj)} = S[i+1] * P^0 + S[i+2] * P^1 + S[i+3] * P^2 + ... + S[i+N] * P^{N-1}$

Now, consider this: $\mathbf{H(Sj) * P}$

$\mathbf{H(Sj) * P} = S[i+1] * P^1 + S[i+2] * P^2 + S[i+3] * P^3 + ... + S[i+N] * P^N$

This is same as $\mathbf{H(Si) + S[i] * P^0 - S[i+N] * P^N}$

So, $\mathbf{H(Sj) * P = H(Si) + S[i] * P^0 - S[i+N] * P^N}$

Hence, if you have calculated the integer or hash value of the previous substring, you can calculate the hash value for the next substring in constant time provided:

- You have precomputed power values like P^N

This is an important concept as it is taking you linear time O(N) to compute the hash value of the first substring and following it, it is taking O(1) constant time for each substring. Hence, the time complexity of converting all sub-strings to integers is O(N).

This is an important concept. Think about this deeply.

This concept is known as rolling hash and you should read more about it here: https://iq.opengenus.org/rolling-hash/

With this, the idea of solving our problem boils down to following steps:

- Convert each substring to hash value using rolling hash
- For each substring, compare the hash value to the hash value of search string
- If it matches, the string has been found
- If not, move on to the next substring unless the end of string is reached

Note that we have reduced the time complexity to linear time **O(N)**. A key thing to note here is that the general steps are the same as our initial approach but for each individual step, we changed our strategy and improved the overall performance.

The pseudocode of this approach will be as follows:

```
hashmap defined
int length1 = length(string1), length2 = length(string2)
power_int = 3, power = 1, hash = 0
for i from 0 to length2-1
    hash = hash + string1[i] * power
    power = power * power_int
hashmap.add(hash)
new_hash = 0
for i from length2 to length1-length2+1
    new_hash = hash - string1[i-length2] ) / power_int + string1[i] *
power
    hashmap.add(new_hash)

hash_substring = 0, power = power_int
for i from 0 to length2
    hash_substring += string2[i] * power
    power = power * power_int

if hash_substring is in hashmap
    substring found
```

Go through this problem once again as it is the foundation of solving string-based problems. If you can understand this deeply, you will be able to solve any string-based problems.

Go through these articles to build upon your knowledge and ask us questions so that we can clarify it:

- Rolling hash: iq.opengenus.org/rolling-hash/ by Ashutosh Singh at OpenGenus
- String hashing: iq.opengenus.org/string-hashing/ by OpenGenus
- Check longest common sub-string using rolling hash: iq.opengenus.org/longest-common-substring-using-rolling-hash/ by Ashutosh Singh at OpenGenus

Take some rest and then, move to the next problem which is an optimization problem.

We just solved a foundational string-based problem. Enjoy.

Problem 2: Longest Common Substring

String problems are fundamental as it has properties distinct from numeric data. A common approach is to convert string to corresponding numeric data and work on it accordingly. In some problems, working on string data directly turns out to be efficient. We will explore **this idea of working on string data directly**.

This is an **important problem** as we will see how a simple approach (involving string manipulation ideas) has the same time complexity as the Dynamic Programming approach but in practice, Dynamic Programming approach is much faster.

Let us understand our current problem.

A substring is a contiguous sequence of characters within a string. For example, **open** is a substring of **opengenus**. Given two strings say S1 and S2, we need to find a string S3 which is a substring to both S1 and S2. We need to find the longest such string S3.

Let us understand this problem with examples.

Examples:

- S1 = opengenus
- S2 = genius
- S3 = gen

The longest common substring of str1 (opengenus) and str2 (genius) is "gen" of length 3. Other common substrings are "us", "g", "ge", "en" and much more.

"gen" is the longest such substring and hence, "gen" is the answer.

- S1 = carpenter
- S2 = sharpener
- S3 = arpen

The longest common substring of str1 (carpenter) and str2 (sharpener) is "arpen" of length 5.

Pause and think for a couple of minutes before proceeding further

---

Following is the summary of the approaches we will take one by one:

- Brute force **O(N⁴) time, O(1) space**
- Hashing approach **O(N²) time, O(N²) space**

- Dynamic Programming **O(N²) time, O(N) space**

The brute force approach to solve this is to generate all substrings of the first string S1 and for each substring, we need to check if it is a substring of the second string S2 as well. This way we need to maintain the length of the longest substring.

Steps:

- Set largest to 0
- For each substring A1 of string S1
  - Check if A1 is a substring of string S2 by comparing with all substrings of S2 of length L (length of substring A1)
  - If yes, check if its length is > largest, then set largest to length

This process takes $O(N^4)$ time for strings of length N as:

- There are $O(N^2)$ substrings of a string of length N
- There are $O(N)$ substrings of a given length L
- It takes $O(N)$ time to compare two strings of length N

Pseudocode:

```
S1 = string of length N
S2 = string of length M

for i from 0 to N
    for j from i to N
        substring = substring in S1 from i to j
```

```
for k from 0 to M-(j-i+1)
    check = 1
    for l from k to k+(j-i+1)
        if S1.char(l) != S1.char(i+l-k)
            check = 0
            break
        if (check == 1 and result < (j-i+1))
            result = j-i+1

result is our answer
```

We can improve this brute force by the simple idea that:

"Strings can be transformed to Numeric data"

This will result in comparing strings in constant time O(1) instead of O(N) linear time.

The key idea of this approach is to convert strings to an integer using String hashing techniques so that the comparison time reduces to constant time O(1). This will bring the overall time complexity to O(N2).

Steps:

- For each substring of S1, generate hash and store it in a hashmap

- For each substring of S2, check if it exists in the hashmap and keep track of the longest substring.

Note that generating hash of a string of length N takes O(N) time. In this view, the overall time complexity stays $O(N^3)$ as there are $O(N^2)$ substrings.

This can be overcome as we can use the rolling hash technique to compute the hashing. The key idea is to use the hash of the previous substring to generate the hash of the next substring where only constant number of characters change. This results in O(N) time complexity for N strings that is constant average time O(1).

Steps:

- For each substring of S1, generate hash and store it in a hashmap using rolling hash technique
- For each substring of S2, check if it exists in the hashmap and keep track of the longest substring.

This brings the **time complexity to $O(N^2)$**.

We covered this point along with concepts like rolling hash in detail in the 4th problem in our book:

Problems for the day before your coding interview by Aditya Chatterjee & Ue Kiao (OpenGenus).

Problems
for the day
before your
coding interview

By Aditya Chatterjee & Ue Kiao

OpenGenus.org

Find it on Amazon: **daybefore1.opengenus.org**

We will solve this problem using a Dynamic Programming approach. The time complexity will be same as our previous approach but in practice, this **Dynamic Programming approach** is much faster as it minimizes several operations.

This will be faster as it has less memory requirements than our previous hashing approach. The space complexity of **hashing approach** is $O(N^2)$ while our **Dynamic Programming** has space complexity as $O(2 \times N) = O(N)$.

Let the first string be s1 and second be s2. Suppose we are at DP state when the length of s1 is i and length of s2 is j, the result of which is stored in dp[i][j]. So, it means:

```
dp[i][j] = length of the longest substring in first i
           characters of S1 and first j characters of S2
```

Now if s1[i-1] == s2[j-1], then dp[i][j] = 1 + dp[i-1][j-1],

The recursive relation to compute the elements of the above DP array is as follows:

If the character at i^{th} position of S1 is same as j^{th} character of S2, then the longest substring considering first i characters of S1 and j characters of S2 is same as 1 + longest substring considering first i characters of S1 and j characters of S2.

Think of this carefully.

Following is the relation:

```
dp[i][j] = 1 + dp[i-1][j-1]   if s1[i-1] == s2[j-1]
```

To print the longest common substring, we use variable end. When dp[i][j] is calculated, it is compared with res where res is the maximum length of the common substring.

If res is less than dp[i][j], then end is updated to i-1 to show that longest common substring ends at index i-1 in s1 and res is updated to dp[i][j]. The longest common substring then is from index end – res + 1 to index end in s1.

Following is the pseudocode of our approach:

```
dp[][] = 2D array N x M
result = 0, r = 0, c = 0

for i from 0 to M + 1
   for j from 0 to N + 1
      if (i == 0 or j == 0)
         dp[i][j] = 0
      else if (S1[i-1] == S2[j-1])
         dp[i][j] = dp[i-1][j-1] + 1
         if (result < dp[i][j])
         {
            result = dp[i][j];
            r = i;
            c = j;
         }
      else
         dp[i][j] = 0

result is our answer
```

The basic condition of calculating dp[][] is result of current row in matrix dp[][] depends on values from previous row. Hence the required length of longest common substring can be **obtained by maintaining values of two consecutive rows only**, thereby reducing space requirements to **O(2 * N)**.

This would result in the following pseudocode:

```
dp[][] = 2D array 2 x M
result = 0, r = 0, c = 0
current = 0

for i from 0 to M + 1
    for j from 0 to N + 1
        if (i == 0 or j == 0)
            dp[current][j] = 0
        else if (S1[i-1] == S2[j-1])
            dp[current][j] = dp[current-1][j-1] + 1
            if (result < dp[current][j])
            {
                result = dp[current][j];
                r = i;
                c = j;
            }
        else
            dp[current][j] = 0
        current = 1 - current

result is our answer
```

Example

For instance, if we consider string doll as str1 and another string dog as str2 and loop through all characters of str1,position denoted by i, and str2,position denoted by j, to build the table dp[][].

We consider the variable curr to state the current row which toggles its value to 0 and 1 at the end of every outer iteration.

When i=0 we all the values of dp[][] corresponding to the first row is set 0.When i=1 and str1[i-1]!=str2[j-1], dp[curr][j] = 0.

When str1[i-1] = str2[j-1] = 'd' (at j=1) , dp[cur][j] = dp[1][1] = dp[1-curr][j-1] + 1 = 0+1 =1. We store the maximum length of longest common substring (maximum value of dp[cur][j]) as res and the ending index of the substring as end. Here res=1 and end=0.

When i=2 and j=2, curr=0, str1[i-1] = 'o' and str2[j-1] = 'o'.Since str1[i-1] = str2[j-1] therefore dp[curr][j] = dp[1-curr][j-1] + 1 = dp[1][1] + 1 = 1 + 1 = 2.

Since res = 1 which is less than dp[curr][j], res = dp[curr][j] = 2 and end = i-1 = 1.

All other positions of dp is less than res. So, finally the length of the largest common substring between doll and dog is 2.

To retrieve the substring iterate from position end-res+1 i.e. 1-2+1 = 0 till end i.e. 1 in str1 doll to get do as the largest common substring between dog and doll.

Since we are using two for loops for both the strings, therefore the time complexity of finding the longest common substring using dynamic programming approach is **O(N * M)** where n and m are the lengths of the strings. Since this implementation involves only two rows and n columns for building dp[][],therefore, the space complexity would be **O(2 * N)**.

Hence, this problem demonstrates the strength of Dynamic Programming approach. Following is the summary of the approaches:

- Brute force **O(N⁴) time, O(1) space**
- Hashing approach **O(N²) time, O(N²) space**
- Dynamic Programming **O(N²) time, O(N) space**

Think of the approaches deeply as it gives deep insights on the link of Dynamic Programming and Hashing techniques.

Go through these articles to build upon your knowledge on this problem and ask us questions so that we can clarify it:

- Rolling hash: iq.opengenus.org/rolling-hash/ by Ashutosh Singh at OpenGenus

- String hashing: iq.opengenus.org/string-hashing/ by OpenGenus
- Check longest common sub-string using rolling hash: iq.opengenus.org/longest-common-substring-using-rolling-hash/ by Ashutosh Singh at OpenGenus

We just solved an important Dynamic Programming approach for string-based problems

Problem 3: Longest repeating sub-string

This is an important problem as in this, we have demonstrated how we can **apply Dynamic programming to a string data**.

The key distinction is that we are **dealing with just 1 string instead of 2 strings** as in the previous problem. Unlike the previous problem, the Dynamic Programming approach is the **only optimal solution**.

If you want to master Dynamic Programming, you should definitely read our **Dynamic Programming book** in this series "**Day before coding Interview**"

Dynamic Programming for the day before your coding interview

Series: Day before coding Interview

We have to find the **longest repeating and non-overlapping substring** in a given string. A substring is a contiguous sequence of characters within a string. We have to return the substring of maximum length which occurs more than once in the string without any overlap. We can return any such substring if more than one such substring exists in the string.

Before going into the solutions, let us go through some examples to understand the problem better.

```
Input:  largelargerlargest
Output:  large

Input:  banana
Output:  an  or  na

Input:  opengenus
Output:  en

Input: aaaaaa
Output: aaa
```

Before proceeding further, think of this problem carefully.

The two approaches we will explore are:

- Brute force **O(N³) time**
- Dynamic Programming **O(N²) time**

Naive Approach

We can solve the problem in **O(N³) time-complexity** by finding all substrings in $O(N^2)$ and checking it with the substrings of the remaining string in $O(N)$.

If we do not consider the condition of "**non-overlapping substrings**", then the problem is easy to solve. We can simply get all sub-strings and store it in a hash map with corresponding element as the count. At the end, we need to get the sub-string will the maximum count (which can be tracked from the beginning).

Steps:

- H is empty hash map, max = 0 and max_string = ""
- For every substring S1 of string S:
  - If S1 is in H, increment the value of S1 (H[S1]++)
  - If S1 is not in H, add it to H with value 1 (H[S1] = 1)
  - If max < H[S1]
    - Set max = H[S1] and max_string = S1
- max_string is our answer

This approach takes **O(N²) time**.

The problem with the above approach is that **it is counting sub-strings which overlap and this can result in wrong answers**. Consider this case of overlapping substrings:

S = "aaaaa"

Substring from index 0 to 2 = "aaa"
Substring from index 2 to 4 = "aaa"

Both sub-strings are same but are overlapping and hence, cannot be considered. Our current approach considers it.

The solution is to modify our native approach to keep track of overlapping substrings.

A simple solution is to compare a substring with all other substring of the same size and keep a track of substrings which are same and are not overlapping.

Steps:

- For substring S1 in string S:

- o L = length of S1
- o For substring S2 of length L in S:
  - If S1 == S2 and S1 and S2 does not overlap (check index):
    - ++count
- o If max < count
  - Max = count
  - Max_string = S1
- Max_string is our answer

The time complexity of this approach is $O(N^3)$ as:

- There are $O(N^2)$ substrings in a string of length N
- There are $O(N)$ substrings of a given length L

The real time performance can be improved if we use a hash map and while generating substrings, we will maintain the count. For overlapping substrings which are same, we will consider this as a collision and use one of the collision handling techniques (like using a linked list).

If we encounter a substring will appeared previously, we will, simply, increment the count of all elements in the linked list entry for which the index does not overlap.

In this approach, we need to store the indexes as well so it increases the memory consumption and the space complexity becomes **O(N)**. The time complexity remains **O(N³)** but several operations are reduced in real time.

We will go to the **Dynamic Programming approach** where we will be able to solve this problem in **O(N²)** time and **O(N²)** space.

Dynamic Programming Approach

The central idea is to look for every same character and save its index.

Check whether difference between index is less than longest repeating and non-overlapping substring size.

We will define **dp[i][j]** which stores the length of the matching and non-overlapping substrings ending with i^{th} and j^{th} characters.

```
dp[i][j] = length of match and non-overlapping substrings
           ending with i-th and j-th characters (two occurrence)
```

Hence, the answer is the maximum value in the matrix dp.

The substring is from index **"i – dp[i][j]" to "i"**

If the characters at $(i-1)^{th}$ and $(j-1)^{th}$ position matches dp[i-1][j-1] is less than the length of the considered substring (j-1) then maximum value of dp[i][j] and the maximum index i till this point is updated. The length of the longest repeating and non-overlapping substring can be found by the maximum value of dp[i][j] and the substring itself can be found using the length and the ending index which is the finishing index of the suffix.

```
if(str[i-1] == str[j-1] && dp[i-1][j-1] < (j - i))
{
    dp[i][j] = dp[i-1][j-1] + 1;
}
```

For Example:

Consider the word **banana**:

Try to follow the process and fill the following Dynamic Programming table:

The final matrix dp[][] would be:

J=0	1	2	3	4	5	6
i=0	.	.	.	.	.	.
1	.	.	.	.	.	.
2	.	.	.	.	.	.
3	.	.	.	.	.	.
4	.	.	.	.	.	.
5	.	.	.	.	.	.
6	.	.	.	.	.	.

Before we fill in the matrix, let us go through the pseudocode:

```
index = 0, length = 0

if(str[i-1] == str[j-1] && dp[i-1][j-1] < (j - i))
{
    dp[i][j] = dp[i-1][j-1] + 1;

    if (dp[i][j] > length)
    {
        length = dp[i][j];
        index = MAXIMUM(i, index);
    }
}
else
    dp[i][j] = 0;

answer is substring from index "index-length+1" to "index"
```

Let us follow the pseudocode and fill the matrix:

The only matching characters are "**a**" (2nd, 4th and 6th) and "**n**" (3rd and 5th). Hence, for all other indices i, dp[i][j]=0.

Initially finishing index index=0 and maximum length of substring length=0.

When i=2 and j=4,

Since, dp[i-1][j-1]=0 which is less than (j-i) i.e. 2,

   dp[i][j] = dp[i-1][j-1]+1 ,

i.e.,dp[2][4]=1.

As dp[2][4] > len

   length = dp[2][4]=1

   index = maximum(index , i)=2

When i=2 and j=6,

Since dp[i-1][j-1]=dp[1][5]=0 which is less than (j-i) i.e. 4,

   dp[i][j]=dp[i-1][j-1]+1 ,

i.e.,dp[2][6]=1.

As dp[2][6] = length,

   length and index would not be updated.

When i=4 and j=6,

Since dp[i-1][j-1]=dp[3][5]=0 which is less than (j-i) i.e. 2,

   dp[i][j]=dp[i-1][j-1]+1 ,

i.e.,dp[4][6]=1.

As dp[4][6]=length,

   length and index would not be updated.

When i=3 and j=5,

Since dp[i-1][j-1]=dp[2][4]=1 which is less than (j-i) i.e. 2,

　dp[i][j]=dp[i-1][j-1]+1 ,

i.e., dp[3][5]=2.

As dp[3][5] > length

　length = dp[3][5]=2

　index = maximum(index, i)=3

The final matrix dp[][] would be:

J=0	1	2	3	4	5	6
i=0 0	0	0	0	0	0	0
1 0	0	0	0	0	0	0
2 0	0	0	0	1	0	1
3 0	0	0	0	0	2	0
4 0	0	0	0	0	0	1
5 0	0	0	0	0	0	0
6 0	0	0	0	0	0	0

To retrieve the longest repeating and non-overlapping substring, we store the characters present from position (index-length+1) till position (index), i.e, the substring from position 2 till position 3 giving the substring an as the result.

Our string was "**banana**" so the substring is "**na**"

Complexity

The time and space complexity of our Dynamic Programming approach are:

- Worst case time complexity: **O(N²)**
- Average case time complexity: **O(N²)**
- Best case time complexity: **O(N²)**
- Space complexity: **O(N²)**

Building a 2D table requires two for loops hence the time-complexity of this algorithm will be **O(N²)**. Also making a 2D table would require N^2 space hence the space complexity of this algorithm will also be **O(N²)**.

In terms of space complexity, we observe the following points:

- Brute force approach has constant space requirements O(1)
- Optimized version of our brute force approach using hash map has $O(N^2)$ space requirement
- Our Dynamic Programming approach improves the time complexity by a factor of O(N) and has space requirement of $O(N^2)$.

As we see, we have been able to solve this string problem using Dynamic Programming in **O(N²)** from **O(N³)** of Brute force approach.

The key takeaways are:

- Take each character as endpoints to formulate a Dynamic Programming approach
- Strings are usually seen as a 2D data

This defines the foundation of handling multi-dimensional data. Strings can be seen as 2 dimensional data and can be converted to 1 dimensional data as we demonstrated in our first problem.

We, just, solved a challenging string problem using Dynamic Programming

---

With this problem, we have come to the end of the short guide on String Algorithms. Think about the above problems deeply as it captures several insights which will enable you to solve problems using approaches as well.

iq.opengenus.org

 discuss.opengenus.org

 team@opengenus.org

 amazon.opengenus.org

 linkedIn.opengenus.org

 github.opengenus.org

 twitter.opengenus.org

 facebook.opengenus.org

 instagram.opengenus.org

Feel free to get in touch with us and enjoy learning and solving computation problems.

www.ingramcontent.com/pod-product-compliance
Lightning Source LLC
LaVergne TN
LVHW081807050326
832903LV00027B/2132